GROSS
PLACES

Pete Jenkins

D1404586

Guided Reading Level: U

Rourke
Educational Media
rourkeeducationalmedia.com

Scan for Related Titles and
Teacher Resources

An abanoned surgical center at the Pripyat hospital in northern Ukraine, inside the Chernobyl exclusion zone.

TABLE OF CONTENTS

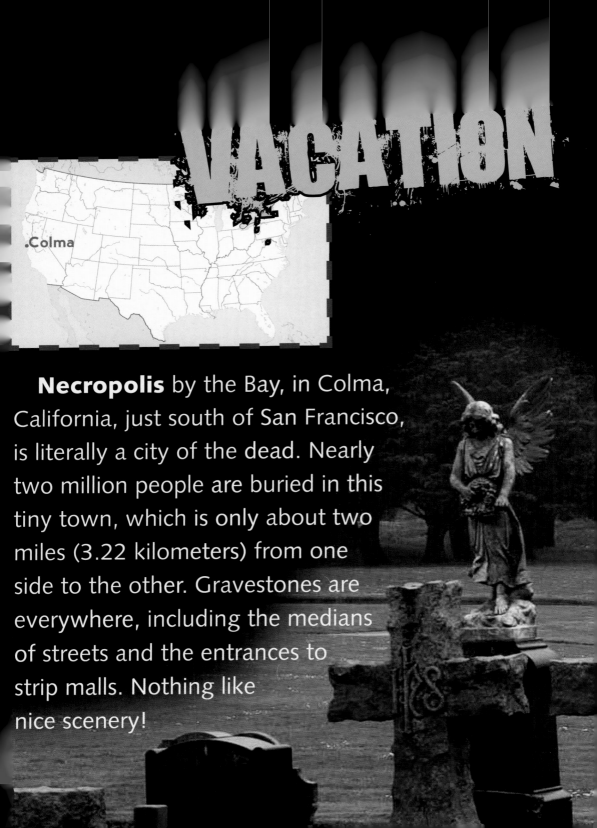

VACATION

.Colma

Necropolis by the Bay, in Colma, California, just south of San Francisco, is literally a city of the dead. Nearly two million people are buried in this tiny town, which is only about two miles (3.22 kilometers) from one side to the other. Gravestones are everywhere, including the medians of streets and the entrances to strip malls. Nothing like nice scenery!

DESTINATIONS

Founded in 1924 as the largest necropolis in the country, the town's entire future lies in burying and maintaining dead bodies. In this community of 1,800 people, the dead outnumber the living 900 to one.

When land became scarce in San Francisco in early 1900, the buried dead were transferred to Colma. Their families were charged 10 dollars for the move. Those whose relatives couldn't afford the cost were reinterred in unmarked graves.

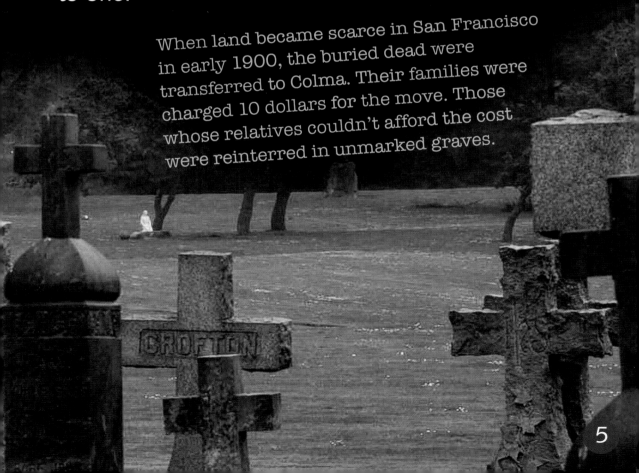

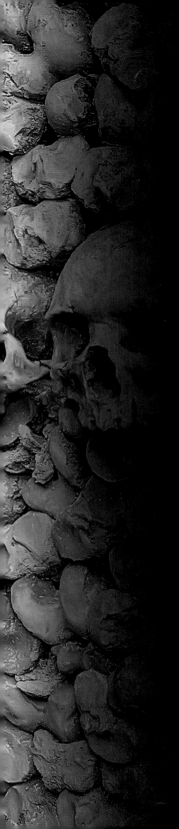

Paris, the capital of France, is often called *La Ville Lumière* (The City of Light), but beneath this busy city of 12 million people lies a dark subterranean world holding the remains of six million of its former **inhabitants**.

The Paris Catacombs is a network of old caves, tunnels, and quarries stretching hundreds of miles, and seemingly lined with the bones of the dead.

The Paris Catacombs are still open to the general public today, although access is limited to a small fraction of the network. It has been illegal since 1955 to enter the other parts of the catacombs. But that doesn't stop Parisians known as Cataphiles from illegally exploring them.

Spooky!

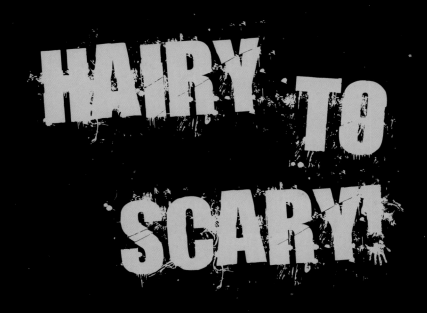

HAIRY TO SCARY!

Leila's Hair Museum in Independence, Missouri, founded in 1989 by former hairdresser Leila Cohoon, contains a multitude of framed hair art. Most are more than a hundred years old. Rings, bracelets, necklaces, earrings, and even buttons made out of hair can all be observed at this strange, hair-raising museum!

Braided hair wreaths are the main attraction, but other human hair is also on **display**, including hair that's been added to portraits and postcards. Creepy portraits of hair glued to baby heads? Now that's just gross!

Creating hair jewelry and art was a feminine way of bonding and grieving.

One corner of the museum displays strands of hair cut from Abe Lincoln and Marilyn Monroe. Another interesting display is of a woman convict's "hair diary." She made all visitors who came to see her while she was imprisoned bring a piece of their hair to add to her diary.

The Karni Mata, or Rat Temple, in India is literally crawling with thousands of these rodents! At this temple, the rats are considered sacred. If you kill one, you have to replace it with a rat made of solid gold. These are some pampered rats!

Karni Mata was part of the Charin clan. She is said to have lived to be 150 years old while remaining youthful and beautiful. After her death, she became a rat. Followers of the clan believe that once they die, they will be reincarnated as a rat and, when a rat dies, it will be reincarnated as a human again.

It's a continuously moving cycle. Kind of like a rat on a wheel!

Visitors to this temple must remove their shoes before entering. It is considered good luck if rats scamper across your feet. Another special sight is that of an albino, or white rat. They are said to be the most sacred of the rats and rarely seen.

There are only four or five white rats out of the 20,000 at the temple. The best time to see the temple is late at night or before sunrise, when the ravenous rodents are out in full force. Only rats within the temple walls are thought to be reincarnated and sacred. The regular street rats are just, well, rats.

BAT POOP AND CREEPY

Bracken Cave, located about 25 miles (40.23 kilometers) northeast of San Antonio, Texas, is a bat-filled wonder. On summer nights, just before sunset, millions and millions of these flying creatures come pouring out of this cave. An estimated 20 million, that is!

CRAWLERS

Mexican free-tailed bats migrate up to 1,000 miles (1,609 kilometers) from their winter home in Mexico to Bracken Cave every March or April. Female bats give birth to one pup. Up to 500 baby bats live crammed into one square foot (30.48 cubic centimeters) of space. All these bats make for a lot of POOP!

Bat poop, called guano, covers the floor. Experts estimate the guano piles to be at least 59 feet (18 meters) deep. That's what 20 million Mexican free-tailed bats can do over hundreds of years.

When adult bats leave the cave at night to feed, they gorge themselves on tons of insects in a single night, including many pests that eat farmers' crops. And they get rid of mosquitoes, too. Their guano also provides food for tiny organisms such as bacteria, fungi, beetles, and flies.

It takes up to three hours for all the bats to emerge from the cave. They make a column so thick it actually shows up on radar at the nearby airport.

BAT FACTS

- Mexican free-tailed bats can fly up to 60 miles (97 kilometers) an hour.
- No other **species** of bat forms as large a colony as the Mexican free-tailed bat.
- Common in central Texas and Mexico, they also live in much of western North America and areas of Central and South America.
- Bats don't always live in caves. They also make their homes in places like mines, tunnels, hollow trees, and under bridges.
- During the Civil War, saltpeter, made from bat guano, was used as an ingredient in gunpowder.

Everyone enjoys a nice autumn hike for fun, but not for fright. Mt. Diablo State Park, located in the San Francisco Bay Area in Northern California, is crawling with tarantulas. You won't need binoculars to find these creepy crawlers!

Tarantula treks, as they are called, are given by tour guides every year from August to October. That's when these furry arachnids come out of their burrows to find a mate. Tarantulas' sizes range from as small as a fingernail to as big as a dinner plate.

All tarantulas are venomous, but only some species have venom strong enough to kill humans. Most bites just cause discomfort and pain for a few days.

You will find these creepy crawlers everywhere at Mt. Diablo. But don't be scared. These carnivores don't eat people. They prefer dining on a variety of insects, especially larger ones such as grasshoppers, crickets, June beetles, caterpillars, and cicadas.

Most tarantula species take two to five years to reach adulthood. After male tarantulas reach maturity, they have about one to one-and-a-half years left to live, and will immediately go in search of a female to mate with. Female tarantulas, on the other hand, have been known to live 30 to 40 years. Now, that's hairy … I mean scary!

DOLLS AND GUM?

Isla de las Munecas (Island of the Dolls) located in the canals south of Mexico City, is home to hundreds of terrifying, **dismembered** dolls. Their severed limbs, decapitated heads, and blank eyes hang from trees, fences, and anywhere else you can think of! Want to play?

More than 50 years ago, Don Julian Santana Barrera found the body of a young girl and her doll floating in the canal. He hung the doll in a tree hoping to appease the ghost of the young girl.

Julian **retreated** to the woods soon after the girl drowned. He claimed he could hear her tormented screams and footsteps in the darkness.

Over the years, he became convinced that the little girl's ghost had possessed the doll and began to hang more and more dolls to try to free her spirit. Since his death in 2001, the area has become a tourist spot where visitors hang up their own dolls.

Julian's relatives now run the area as a tourist attraction and still collect and hang the mutilated dolls. Visitors to the area claim they can hear the dolls whispering to them.

Seattle has a gross attraction known as the Gum Wall. Beginning in the 1990s, patrons would place their chewed-up gum on the wall before entering a show at Post Alley's Market Theater. Piece by piece, it began to expand down the brick alleyway until more than 2,200 pounds (998 kilograms) of gum littered the wall.

The **stench** of decaying chewing gum can be a bit stinky, but the Gum Wall is still a popular tourist attraction. Though considered littering by some, many people think the Gum Wall is a beautiful work of art. A sticky work of art, that is!

On November 10, 2015, the Pike Place Market Preservation and Development Authority began a three-day cleaning of the wall. It was the first time the wall was cleaned in 20 years. The very next weekend, locals and tourists started to recreate the wall all over again.

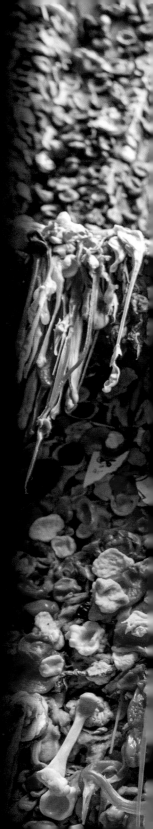

For 2,000 years, the Igorot people of Sagada in the Philippines have put their dead in wooden coffins, then attached the coffins to the side of a cliff to protect the bodies from animals and flooding. That's a lot of bodies! Want to see for yourself? Tour guides lead hikes to the site so you can see the cliff coffins up close.

As you can see, the world is full of some pretty strange places to visit. Some consider them creepy, while others admire their weirdness and unusual scenery. Which one would you like to visit?

All I can say is,

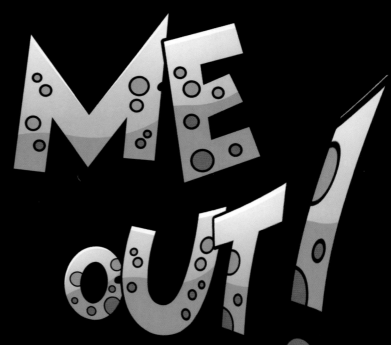

GROSS ME OUT!

GLOSSARY

dismembered (DIS-mem-burhd): to cut off the limbs of a body or animal

display (dis-PLAY): to show or exhibit something

inhabitants (in-HAB-i-tuhnts): people who live in a certain place

necropolis (neh-KROP-oh-liss): a cemetery, especially one in an ancient city

retreated (ri-TREET-id): moved to a quiet place to be alone or isolated

species (SPEE-seez): one of the groups into which animals and plants of the same genus are divided

stench (stench): an offensive odor

temple (TEM-puhl): a building used for worshipping a god or gods

INDEX

SHOW WHAT YOU KNOW

1. Name an item that can be made using bat guano.
2. How many rats are estimated to be in the Karni Mata temple?
3. Why did Don Julian Santana Barrera hang dolls from trees at the Island of the Dolls?
4. How many pounds of gum were estimated to be on the Gum Wall before it was cleaned?
5. How long can a female tarantula live?

WEBSITES TO VISIT

www.kidzworld.com/article/4893-the-worlds-grossest-places

www.viralnova.com/strangest-places-on-earth/

http://well.blogs.nytimes.com/2007/10/31/on-the-web-gross-anatomy-for-kids/?_r=0

Pete Jenkins does not care for rats, creepy dolls, bat caves, hair jewelry, or tarantulas. He does, however, think the Gum Wall is pretty cool! And, on his next trip to Seattle he plans to deposit some of his own gum on the wall. In his travels, he has seen some pretty gross things, from mummy museums to churches filled with bones and skulls of hundreds of bodies. So, we guess he does like to be GROSSED out!

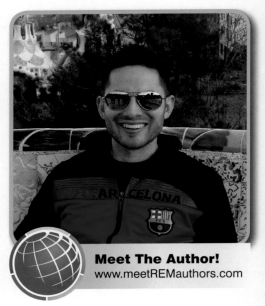

Meet The Author!
www.meetREMauthors.com

© 2017 Rourke Educational Media

www.rourkeeducationalmedia.com

PHOTO CREDITS: Cover: cobwebs © schankz, gum wall © Stockimo, rats © Don Mammoser, Gross Me Out Letters © Cory Thoman all from Shutterstock, dolls © Esparta Palma https://creativecommons.org/licenses/by-sa/4.0/deed.en pages 2-3 © Jakub Kyncl, Shutterstock; page 4-5 map © Uwe Dedering, cemetery © Eden Manus | Dreamstime.com, page 6-7 © Guillermo Pis Gonzalez, inset photo page 6 © Stas Guk both from Shutterstock; page 10-11 rats drinking © Marcel Toung, temple entrance © still, both from Shutterstock; page 12-13 © Don Mammoser, albino rat © George Dolgikh both from Shutterstock; page 14-15 cave entrance © Daniel Spiess https://creativecommons. org/licenses/by-sa/2.0/ flying bats © USFWS/Ann Froschauer; page 16-17 © USFWS/Ann Froschauer; page 18-19 tarantula © Steve Byland Shutterstock, page 20-21 © Angel DiBilio; page 22-25 © Wa17gs, https://creativecommons.org/licenses/by-sa/4.0/deed.en ; page 26-27 © f11photo; Lane V. Erickson, both from Shutterstock; page 28-29 © raphme Shutterstock, Gross Me Out Letters © Cory Thoman Shutterstock

Edited by: Keli Sipperley

Cover and Interior design by: Nicola Stratford   www.nicolastratford.com

Library of Congress PCN Data

Gross Places / Pete Jenkins
(Gross Me Out!)
ISBN 978-1-68191-771-9 (hard cover)
ISBN 978-1-68191-872-3 (soft cover)
ISBN 978-1-68191-960-7 (e-Book)
Library of Congress Control Number: 2016932731

Rourke Educational Media
Printed in the United States of America, North Mankato, Minnesota

Also Available as: